W9-AWQ-407

FIGHT BACK

ALSO BY EMIL FARKAS

The Complete Martial Arts Catalogue
(*with John Corcoran*)

Emil Farkas and
Margaret Leeds

FIGHT BACK

a woman's guide to self-defense

Holt, Rinehart and Winston   New York

Copyright © 1978 by Emil Farkas and Margaret Massey Leeds

All rights reserved, including the right to reproduce this book or portions thereof in any form.

Published simultaneously in Canada by Holt, Rinehart and Winston of Canada, Limited.

Photographs by Emil Farkas.

Library of Congress Cataloging in Publication Data

Farkas, Emil, 1946–
Fight back.

1. Self-defense for women. I. Leeds, Margaret Massey, joint author. II. Title.
GV1111.5.F37   613.6′6   78-2536
ISBN Hardbound 0-03-021051-8
ISBN Paperback 0-03-021056-9

FIRST EDITION

Printed in the United States of America
10 9 8 7 6 5 4 3 2 1

CONTENTS

INTRODUCTION

The purpose of this book is to meet the need for an instruction manual presenting the fundamentals of self-defense in a simple, clear, practical, and easy-to-follow manner. The book is written for both student and instructor: Students may use it in self-programmed study, progressing from the simple to the more advanced techniques; instructors may use it as a guide in organizing and conducting classes in self-defense for girls and women. Finally, it is our hope that this book will serve to answer common questions and dispel many long-lived myths about self-defense for girls and women.

THE FIGHTING ARTS

There are many forms of self-defense: judo, karate, jiujitsu, to name a few. Which martial art is really the best? Each can be deadly when mastered, but the "best" one depends on the ability of the student and the circumstances at the moment of an attack. This manual of practical self-defense combines aspects of many different martial art forms.

Karate (meaning "open hand") is perhaps the most popular form of martial art. It was brought to America in the mid-1950s from Japan and has since been followed by the karate styles from other oriental countries such as Korea, Okinawa, and China. Each style or school offers its own philosophy and training methods, but the ultimate aim of each is the defeat of an enemy. There is, therefore, little difference between one style and another. A karate fighter relies on his hands, elbows, knees, and feet to disable an opponent, whereas those trained in judo and jiujitsu use an opponent's weight to throw him to the ground. Most experts feel that karate is the most effective form of self-defense, as it requires only limited strength and can be used for offense as well as defense.

Kung fu originated in China more than 2,000 years ago. It is more free flowing, more natural looking, more graceful than karate. Because it utilizes softer, less powerful movements, it appeals to the aesthetic sense of many people and is widely studied as an art and a philosophy as well as a means of self-defense. Only recently has this art become popular in America; for many years it was practiced only behind closed doors in the Chinatowns of most major American cities. Kung fu, like karate, uses kicks, punches, and blocks, but kung fu has more movements to be mastered.

Jiujitsu is the oldest Japanese form of self-defense, but in the United States it has lost popularity as the other martial arts have gained. Jiujitsu is a "gentle" art that emphasizes escape techniques from specific holds and throwing and immobilizing an opponent by painful arm and leg locks. Students of jiujitsu learn the vulnerable parts of the body and various means of attacking those parts. As it requires relatively little brute strength, jiujitsu is especially effective for women.

Judo is a Japanese sport similar to jiujitsu and to wrestling. Its techniques consist of throws, pins, and chokes, and because it requires more strength than do the other martial arts, judo is not the best self-defense art for women. Judo was developed by Jigaro Kano, the Japanese jiujitsu expert, who eliminated the rough elements of the jiujitsu techniques and added rules and regulations for contests. Judo is the only martial art in the Olympics, and it is primarily a sport. It can be used as self-defense, but other methods are more practical, because much time and strength are required to attain mastery of judo.

Aikido, unlike judo, kung fu, and karate, is strictly defensive. The stress is placed on being in harmony with your opponent's movements rather than in conflict with them. The art consists of many intricate hand and wrist holds as well as flips; like judo, aikido uses an opponent's strength and weight to his disadvantage. Aikido was founded in Japan about fifty years ago and has been taught in the United States for the past few years. Because it cannot be learned quickly, it has lagged behind the other martial arts in popularity. Recently, however, many women who are philosphically opposed to violence have begun taking up aikido.

There are numerous unorthodox systems of self-defense, including "unarmed combat," "defendo," "kick boxing," "ketsugo." Some have great merit, but the practicality of each depends on the instructor and the student. The greatest difference lies not in what you learn, but in how well you learn it.

If your need is for a practical method of defending yourself, the techniques included in this book will serve you well. If you wish to pursue the martial arts for additional exercise or recreation, the following suggestions may prove helpful:

1. Check with your community center or YWCA. They may offer courses suited to your needs. Not all commercial places teach the best methods.

2. Visit as many martial arts schools as possible. It pays to shop around and compare.

3. Ask how much time you will probably need to invest in order to accomplish your goal. Remember, most schools teach martial arts as a *sport*; to master them for self-defense could take years.

4. Cost is, naturally, an important factor. Investigate the rates in various schools and, if possible, avoid schools that require you to sign a contract.

5. Consider the personality of the instructor with whom you might study. A personality clash can hinder your progress. You also should demand an experienced teacher; many schools assign a high-ranking student to teach beginners. The best performer is not necessarily the best teacher.

6. Talk to students already enrolled; you will often get valuable information from them.

7. Consider the size of the class you might join; the larger the class, the less individual attention you will receive.

8. Concentrate your preliminary investigations on the instructor more than on the school. There are no "good schools," just good instructors.

PREPARING FOR DEFENSE

HOW TO USE THIS BOOK

This manual is organized according to subject matter and technique in order to make it easier to locate specific material and review it mentally. This is not, however, the suggested order in which the techniques should be learned. The schedule of lessons in Appendix 1 presents the recommended progression for learning the skills. To use this book as a home study course in practical self-defense, follow the suggested schedule. Each of your lessons should consist of four parts: discussion, warm-up exercises, new skills, and review.

DISCUSSION

Each lesson should include a discussion or review of important aspects of mental and physical preparation for self-defense, with emphasis on safety precautions. Discussion may come at the beginning or end of the lesson, as you prefer.

WARM-UP EXERCISES

Even though you could not warm up in an emergency situation, it is still important in practice sessions to begin by warming up in order to achieve maximum agility, strength, and flexibility. Always warm up with exercises from each of the three categories described in Chapter 4: Group I, total-body exercises and practice of basic techniques; Group II, strengthening exercises; and Group III, stretching exercises.

NEW SKILLS

After warm-up exercises and basic techniques have been practiced, learn the movement for a new skill and work on it individually. Then practice with a partner, if possible.

REVIEW

Continue to review skills previously learned and to reinforce awareness of the importance of safety precautions.

MENTAL AND PHYSICAL PREPARATION

COMMON SENSE OF SELF-DEFENSE

The best way to defend yourself is to use common sense to avoid dangerous situations. In addition to learning the techniques of self-defense, follow these commonsense guidelines when at home, away from home, walking, driving, and on the telephone.

AT HOME:
1. List only last name and initials on mailboxes and in phone directories.
2. Change the locks after moving into a new home. Pin tumbler or dead-bolt types are best because they are difficult to force.
3. Install and use a chain lock and a peephole. Never open the door to a stranger without having the chain in place.
4. Keep windows secured. Install window locks on those left open for ventilation.
5. If you lose your keys, have the locks changed immediately.
6. Always request a salesman or repairman to show identification before admitting him. If you did not call him, check with the company before admitting him.
7. Do not allow a stranger to enter to use your telephone. Offer to make the call for him instead.
8. Be cautious about entering an elevator with a strange man; it is wiser to wait in the lobby for a few minutes.
9. Stand near the button control panel in an elevator. If you are threatened, push the emergency alarm and as many floor buttons as possible.
10. Do not ride with a strange man in an elevator to the basement or roof or other unsafe area.

11. Do not remain alone in the laundry room of your apartment building.
12. Report suspicious persons, occurrences, or vehicles to the police.
13. If a door or window has been forced or broken while you were absent, *do not enter or call out.* Use a neighbor's phone to call police and wait till they arrive before entering your home. The intruder might still be in there.
14. Keep emergency phone numbers handy in your purse and by your home phone.

AWAY FROM HOME:
1. When you leave home for an extended period of time such as vacation, stop deliveries of newspapers, mail, milk, etc. Do not advertise that you are away.
2. Arrange to have the gardening tended to.
3. Keep drapes and shades closed.
4. Consider installing an automatic control for lights to turn them on and off at night.
5. Make sure all doors and windows are securely locked.
6. Let a neighbor and the police know you will be away so they can keep a watch on your place.
7. Be alert and keep a watch on your neighbor's place when he is away.
8. Always carry some small change with you for emergency phone calls when away from home.

WALKING:
1. Never accept a ride from a stranger.
2. Do not walk alone in an unsafe area or at night if you can avoid it.
3. Walk near the curb and avoid passing close to shrubbery, dark doorways, alleys, or other places that could conceal an attacker. Avoid shortcuts through dark or secluded areas.
4. Have your key ready so you can enter your car or house quickly.
5. If someone suspicious follows you, cross the street. If he follows, ask what he wants and be prepared to defend yourself if he threatens your health or life. If he wants only your possessions, give them to him and prepare to describe him to the police.
6. If a car follows you, turn and walk in the opposite direction.
7. When shopping, avoid carrying a purse whenever possible. If you do carry a purse, wear the shoulder strap across your body diagonally. If you carry a clutch purse, hold it upside down with your hand on the latch so it can be dropped and the contents spilled if a

purse snatcher appears. Never leave your purse in a shopping cart. Never carry more money or credit cards than are necessary, although it's a good idea to have at least $10 to appease a mugger. If your purse is taken with your keys in it, change all locks immediately.

DRIVING:

1. Don't give a ride to a stranger.
2. Keep your car in good working order and have it checked frequently.
3. Don't let the gas tank get below one-quarter full.
4. Keep windows rolled up and doors locked.
5. Try to travel on well-lighted, busy streets.
6. Don't leave your purse on the seat to attract a criminal.
7. If you are threatened and cannot move away, use the horn to draw attention and perhaps scare away the assailant.
8. If you are being followed by another car, do not drive to your home; instead, drive to an open business or the police station.
9. Always write down the license number of any automobile involved in a threat to you and report the incident to the police.
10. If your car becomes disabled in an isolated area, raise the hood, tie a white handkerchief on the antenna, and sit inside your car with windows rolled up and doors locked until help arrives. If a stranger offers help, do not accept a ride; ask him to call for help at the next phone.
11. Do not stop to give aid to a stranger whose car is disabled; send help back to him.
12. Park only in well-lighted spots and look around before leaving your car.
13. Lock your car when you leave it and lock packages in the trunk.
14. Look behind the front seat before entering your car.
15. Look around outside your car before leaving it, particularly at night.
16. Carry your keys on a ring that allows you to separate house keys from car keys so that you don't leave house keys with parking lot attendants or car repairmen.
17. In a bus, sit near the driver if possible.

ON THE TELEPHONE:

1. Notify the police of obscene calls.
2. Never reveal to a stranger over the phone your name or address or even your phone number if it is a wrong-number call.
3. Never admit you are alone, and warn children and baby-sitters not to do so.

4. You might keep a whistle by the phone to hurt the ear of an obscene caller, but be careful the next time you answer the phone, because he could do the same thing to get even.

The Los Angeles Police Department uses the letters of the word SAFE to help women remember the formula for reducing the chance of assault.

S means Secure. Make sure you have good locks; then *use* them.

A means Avoid. Follow the rules of common sense for self-defense outlined above. Avoid placing yourself in potentially dangerous situations. By practicing preventive measures of self-defense, you lessen your chance of having to use physical tactics.

F means Flee. If your preventive measures fail, and you find your health or life is threatened, scream and run if you can reach an area where others can help you. If you cannot reach help, be willing to defend yourself with any means available to you. Talk your way out of the situation if possible. You might begin by asking what the assailant wants. If he wants only your possessions, give them to him and prepare to describe him to the police. If he threatens your health or your life, fight!

E means Escape. Use any means to stop the pursuer. A scream or a loud whistle has proved effective many times to frighten away an attacker or to attract help. Scream "fire, fire, fire" rather than "help," because other people may be more willing to investigate the situation. If you find yourself forced to use physical defense, fight with all your might and all your resources.

REPORTING TO THE AUTHORITIES

If you have been threatened by a robber or an attacker, try to remain calm and observant. Memorize as many of the following characteristics as possible so you can aid the police in identifying him:

Sex	Distinguishing characteristics
Skin color	(scars, etc.)
Age	Physical abnormalities
Height	Speech characteristics
Weight	Clothing
Body build	Mustache or beard
Color of hair	Hair style
Color of eyes	Type of weapon
Shape of nose	In which hand the weapon was held
Teeth	Conversation during the assault

COMMON QUESTIONS AND MYTHS ABOUT SELF-DEFENSE

Do I really need to practice every day for years to make self-defense work for me?
To become a black-belt karate expert requires years of study, but the techniques of practical self-defense presented in this manual are simple, effective, and relatively easy to master.

If I hurt my attacker, won't he just get mad and hurt me worse?
Someone who attacks you physically intends you some harm. If you strike quickly, with accuracy and power, you will not just *hurt* him, you will *disable* him so he cannot strike back.

If I hurt my attacker, am I legally liable?
You have every right to defend yourself against harm. If attacked, go all out in your physical defense. It is the attacker who will have to worry about legal defense. Still, you must use discretion to some extent; once you have disabled your attacker, you should not take it upon yourself to punish him. Leave that to the courts.

Isn't it best just to run away from an attacker?
If you have a head start and a safe place to run where others can help you, then running and screaming may be your best defense. But if you are in an isolated area, a man can probably outrun you and you will have to turn and fight. Remember, too, that you will not always have the option of running; many assaults are surprise attacks in which a woman is grabbed without warning. In that case, fight to disable your attacker and run only when he can no longer pursue.

If someone seems threatening, how close do I let him come before I kick or hit him?
That depends on the situation. If you are walking down the street and a man seems to be following you, cross the street. If he continues to follow you, you can turn and watch his actions. If he approaches and seems to pose a threat, you can begin by asking what he wants. Anytime you can avoid using physical tactics of defense, do so. *Fight only when forced to. Talk your way out whenever possible.* If he moves to make physical contact, kick first and ask questions later.

What if he is really big and strong? I won't have a chance.
Remember to strike at his weak points. There are no exercises to make his *nose* big and strong, and even a big, strong athlete such as a football player is ever fearful of injury to his *knee*. A well-placed strike to the nose and a side kick to the knee can flatten the biggest fellow.

How much should I hurt my attacker?
Make your defense fit the situation. If your "assailant" is an overly amo-
rous date who poses more of an annoyance than a threat, use "gentle per-
suasion" to control the situation. You can use a push under his nose
rather than a palm-heel strike; and you can yank his finger rather than jab
your knee into his groin. But if the person threatens your health or your
life, move to disable him and keep moving until you are safe.

What if I fall down?
You can be just as dangerous from the ground as you are on your feet.
Use your legs to kick and kick and kick. If he is close, strike his nose or
throat.

What if my kicks don't stop him?
Don't expect to rely on one move. It may work, but plan to follow
through with several quick moves. Practice your balance and speed so
you can deliver a series of quick kicks, and practice giving several strikes
in quick succession. If your kicks don't stop him and he is in close, strike
his nose or chin or throat. Work on numerous combinations of moves.

What if I can't get into a good fighting stance?
You may not have enough warning to assume a stance, but balance is
important. Practice shifting weight and changing direction so you can
move quickly and maintain balance even if you are not in a conventional
fighting stance. A fighting stance merely gives you the best ready position for any move.

I practiced choke releases with my boyfriend last night and they didn't work.
One of the most important aspects of your self-defense is the *element of
surprise*. Because most women are weaker than most men, surprise is
very important for the woman. When you are practicing, your partner
knows you will attempt some defensive move. He may not know exactly
what you plan; but because he expects something, he is ready for it and
will be more effective in counteracting it. Also, you will not intentionally
cause your boyfriend pain or injury in order to be successful because you
do not really feel threatened. Your partner in practice situations must use
his imagination when you simulate a wounding tactic. If a man receives
a swift knee to the groin, he is usually less willing to maintain a strong
bear hug.

When I practice the blocking techniques, I hurt my own arm.
A hard block can cause pain, but it is better to hurt your arm a little by
blocking a blow you cannot dodge than to take the force of the blow in
your face, for example. Better to hurt your arm than some more vital area.

You can use batakas or arm pads when practicing blocking, and if you feel a little discomfort, let that remind you that you are better off dodging a blow than blocking it. Block only when you have no other choice.

What if I am attacked by someone who knows karate or self-defense himself?
The chance of your being attacked by an expert in the martial arts is unlikely. Muggers and rapists don't usually join karate schools; they get their exercise elsewhere. Nevertheless, if the improbable happens, you can still rely on the element of surprise: He will not expect you to be trained in self-defense, so make your move quickly and follow through with counterattacks to the best of your ability. There is never any guarantee that you will win, but you stand a better chance if you try.

What if I am attacked by more than one man?
Obviously, two opponents are more dangerous than one, but you can still benefit from the element of surprise if you move quickly. Make every kick and strike count, and keep moving and screaming. Again, you may not win; but if they mean to harm you, you can at least try to prevent it.

What if the attacker has a weapon?
If an armed attacker wants only your possessions, give them up. No object or amount of money is worth your life. If he intends to do you bodily harm, then use your head first and try to talk your way out. If that doesn't work, you have at least bought a little time to gather your wits and plan what to do next. There are defenses you can use against a knife, but they take quick action and plenty of practice. *If the weapon is a gun, never try to fight.* Only comic book characters are faster than a speeding bullet. Try to remain calm and avoid sudden moves or sounds. Don't startle your assailant into pulling the trigger unintentionally. Try to avoid looking at the gun. Look at the person and concentrate on describing him accurately to the police.

If I use my keys or comb or something in my purse to defend myself, am I guilty of carrying a concealed weapon?
Simple objects are not considered weapons from a legal standpoint. Problems arise with the use of a gun, a switchblade knife, or such things as a can of Mace, but don't worry about using common objects. They can be of great help in an emergency. Police usually advise a woman not to rely on a gun or knife because of the risk of being disarmed and supplying the attacker with a weapon he would not otherwise have had.

Should I fight an unarmed robber to protect my valuables?
Realize that an "unarmed" robber may have a concealed weapon. You have to decide which is more important—your well-being or your pos-

sessions. If you are victimized by a purse snatcher who grabs and runs, don't pursue: Spend your energies closing credit card accounts and changing locks. If you find yourself on one end of the purse strap and a thief on the other, a swift kick to the knee or groin should loosen his grip, but the basic rule is *fight only when your health is threatened.* You may be unhappy about the loss of your purse, but be glad if that is your biggest loss.

What if he tries to rape me? Should I fight or submit as long as he doesn't start beating me?
As always, consider the situation and use your intuition. *Try to talk your way out first.* If you look young enough, you might tell him you are only seventeen years old. This has worked in some instances. His desire may wane when he thinks of a charge of statutory rape. If you can't talk your way out and you can't escape, then you will have to fight if you want to prevent the rape. Convicted rapists, when interviewed in prison, have advised that a woman not resist a rapist because she runs a greater risk of being seriously hurt or killed. But then, consider the source. Rapists are not known for their desire to help women in rape attacks.

I would rather practice nonviolence; I don't want to hurt another person.
You may have only the option of hurting him or allowing him to harm you. Your move is defensive; his is offensive. Which is more acceptable to you?

What if I can't remember the right moves to make in a particular situation?
You practice certain routines to improve your agility, your ability, and your versatility in defensive moves, not to restrict yourself to specific routines. *There are no rules. If it works for you, it's right!*

PSYCHOLOGICAL ASPECTS OF SELF-DEFENSE

1. *Be willing to act!* Your chance for success is determined by your attitude. If attacked, fight back. If someone has to be hurt, let it be the attacker.

2. *Don't be an easy victim. Shout! Resist! Fight!* Statistics show that in 60 percent of attacks against women, the woman escapes unharmed by merely screaming.

3. *Use the element of surprise.* As soon as you shout and resist, the element of surprise is on your side. Your attacker does not expect effective resistance. Move quickly and keep using defensive tactics until you control the situation.

4. *Develop self-confidence.* Believe in your own ability to use these simple self-defense techniques. Practice until your response is automatic.

5. *Believe in what you are doing.* Act with determination. These techniques *do work*, and they can work for you.

6. *Don't panic.* If you can't control yourself, you can't control the situation.

7. *Bluff.* Make an effort to show your attacker you are not afraid. Concentrate on winning.

8. *Escape.* Your first inclination may be to run, but run only if there is a safe place nearby where other people can help you. If there's nobody to help you, run only after you have made sure the attacker cannot pursue.

9. *Keep it simple.* You are not out to dazzle anyone with a slick routine. Stick to those techniques you can use easily and quickly.

10. *Don't hesitate.* Once you are forced to defend yourself, use everything available to you: Shout, strike, kick, throw something, bite. If you start a defense, *finish* it.

11. *Know yourself.* Don't have *two* strangers to deal with in the attack. Know yourself and know your capabilities. Be prepared to use everything you know you can do, and if that is not enough, be prepared to improvise.

12. *Don't expect to fight gently; an attacker is no gentleman.*

THE VOICE AS A WEAPON

Don't let the attacker scare you speechless; your voice can be one of your most effective weapons. Use it! Your voice can serve multiple purposes.

Try to *talk* your way out of a threatening situation. Always do all within your power to avoid a physical confrontation with an attacker. Anytime you fight with an attacker, there is the chance he can win. Even a black-belt karate expert is not invincible. You may be confronted by someone who is not rational; maybe he is psychotic or on drugs and cannot be reasoned with. Use your voice to try to calm him, to soothe him, to reassure *him* that *you* are no threat. Perhaps you can remove the threat of violence by changing the atmosphere of the confrontation—and then again maybe you can't. But you have lost nothing by trying. *Never fight a man unless forced to in order to protect your health!*

Screaming startles your attacker and may attract other people to help you. Statistics have shown that in 60 percent of attacks on women, the woman escapes unharmed if she screams. Don't scream "help, help,

help!" Scream "fire, fire, fire!" Many people hesitate to get involved in another person's troubles or are afraid to risk getting hurt themselves. If you yell "fire," though, the instinct for survival tells others they may already be involved in your problem; it becomes their problem, and they are more inclined to investigate. If you were sitting at home watching television one evening and you heard a woman screaming for help, you might hesitate and debate before responding. But if you heard a woman yelling "fire!" you would make a dash for the door to see if the alarm should be yours. One reminder here: If a knife or a gun is held on you, don't yell or make sudden movements. You don't want to make your attacker any more nervous than he probably already is.

Shout upon impact when kicking and striking: It adds power. Shouting when you are kicking and striking makes you appear more vicious to your attacker and a much less willing victim. It can break his concentration long enough to allow you to deliver the kick or strike that ends the fight. Shouting also helps to give you more power behind the kick or strike. You cannot scream loudly without tightening your stomach muscles to force the sound out. Practice coordinating the force of the shout with the force of the blow and you will have added power. Shout "KIA-A-A-H!" *Don't rely on being able to shout without practicing. Practice until shouting is an easy thing for you to do and is automatic with your kicks and strikes.*

3.

NATURAL WEAPONS AND TARGET AREAS

NATURAL WEAPONS

Your body is loaded with natural weapons. *Legs* are longer and stronger than arms and can kick in all directions. Feet are stronger than hands; use them for kicking and stomping. Your knee can give powerful blows when in close.

Your *arms* can be used to block and to attack. Your palm heel can strike. Your fist (the side, not the knuckles) can punch. Your elbow can hit hard to the ribs, face, and stomach. Your fingers can jab, poke, scratch (but should be used only as a last resort, as they are tender).

Body movement makes your chances of self-defense better; a moving target is harder to hit or to grab. Shoulders can push your attacker off balance. Body weight propelled toward an attacker can throw him off balance.

Head butting can cause pain. Biting can also cause pain, distract an attacker, and make him relax his grip or his concentration.

Your *voice*, as we've mentioned, is a powerful weapon. Shout to distract the attacker and perhaps scare him away or attract other people to help. And shout upon contact during counterattack, using noises that make you sound fierce.

Your *brain* is the most important natural weapon. It directs the whole show. Use it to size up your opponent, to survey the situation, to act with calm control and with forceful determination, and to improvise when necessary. Keep thinking!

PRESSURE POINTS AND TARGET AREAS

Just as your body is loaded with natural weapons, your opponent's body is loaded with weak spots and vulnerable areas. Pages 20–21 show thirty target areas, front and back, as well as the kinds of techniques that can be applied to them.

Learn to *strike at your opponent's weak spots.* A man can tense his stomach muscles to make that area less vulnerable to pain, but he can't tense his nose or his knees. So a well-aimed blow to his nose or knee is more effective than punching away at his stomach or hammering your fists against his chest. No matter how big or how strong, every man has his weak spots; concentrate your energies where you can do enough damage to make him leave you alone. It takes only a few pounds of pressure to dislocate a knee, and a well-aimed side kick can have more than enough power to bring an attacker to his knees.

Practice for accuracy. If a man threatens you with serious physical harm, don't rely on stopping him by merely causing him a little discomfort or pain. Be prepared to disable him. You can cause him pain by slapping his face, scratching his cheek, or kicking his shin, but you can disable him by a palm-heel strike to the nose, an elbow to the jaw, a side kick to the knee, or a front kick to the groin. But if you cannot hit a target with your strikes and kicks, you sacrifice effectiveness—and maybe yourself—to that inaccuracy. You won't disable the knee if your kick lands on the thigh, so practice and practice and practice.

Be careful when practicing with a partner. When sparring, never make contact with your kicks or strikes; your partner's pressure points won't know you didn't mean to hurt them. Make full contact only when working against pads.

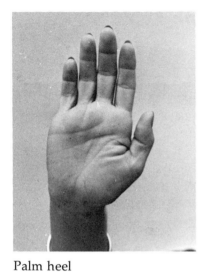

Palm heel

Side of fist

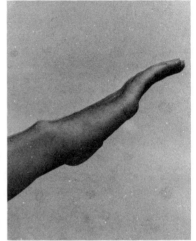

Edge of hand

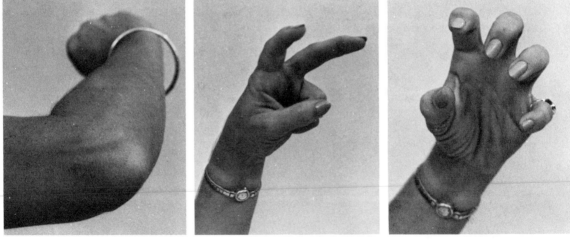

Elbow

Fingers

Fingernails

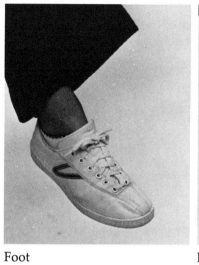

Foot

Knee

Heel

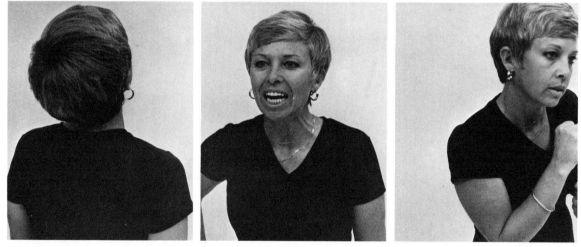

Head

Teeth

Shoulder

SIMPLE OBJECTS AS WEAPONS

Jab or slash with keys.

Jab with rolled-up magazine or newspaper.

Jab with edge of book.

Jab with rat-tail comb or brush or slash with teeth of comb.

Jab with broom or mop handle.

Jab with pencil or pen.

Slash with edge of credit card.

Jab with edge or clasp side of purse.

Strike with sweater or jacket to distract attacker.

Throw dirt into eyes if you are on the ground.

Sling your shoe to distract attacker.

Jab with umbrella.

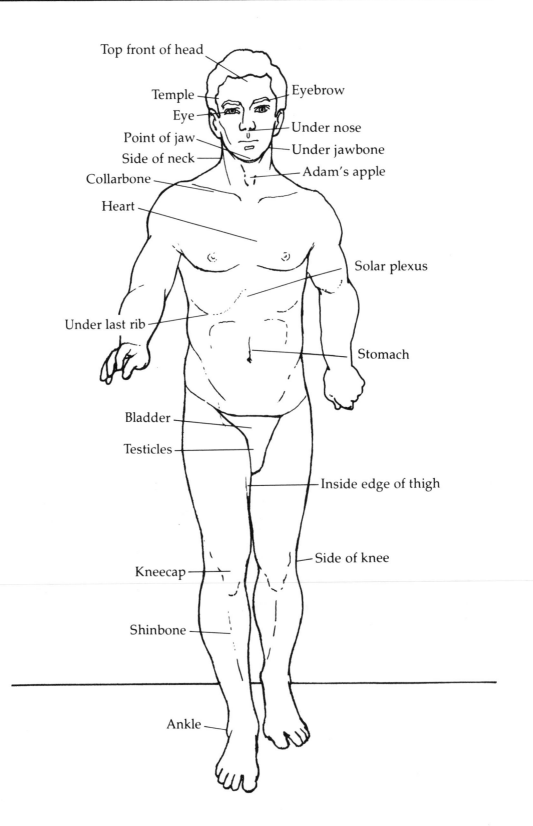

Top front of head

Temple

Eye

Point of jaw

Side of neck

Collarbone

Heart

Under last rib

Bladder

Testicles

Kneecap

Shinbone

Ankle

Eyebrow

Under nose

Under jawbone

Adam's apple

Solar plexus

Stomach

Inside edge of thigh

Side of knee

TARGET AREAS: BACK

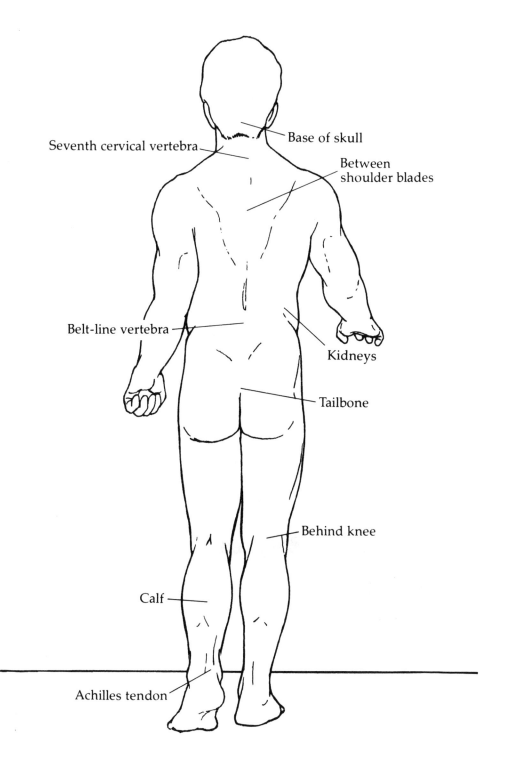

Seventh cervical vertebra

Base of skull

Between
shoulder blades

Belt-line vertebra

Kidneys

Tailbone

Behind knee

Calf

Achilles tendon

TECHNIQUES APPLIED TO PRESSURE POINTS

Pulling hair back from hairline

Side-of-fist strike to temple

Jabbing eyes with fingers

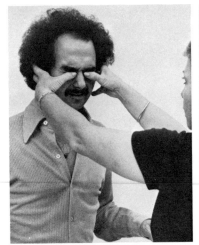
Gouging eyes with thumbs

Palm-heel strike to nose

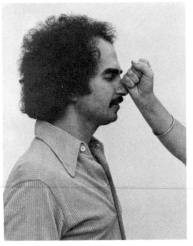
Side-of-fist strike to nose

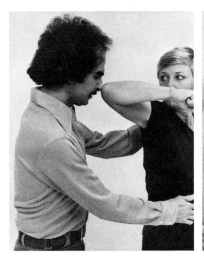

Elbow strike to nose

Knee to nose

Popping ears with both hands

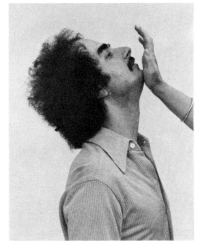

Palm-heel strike to chin

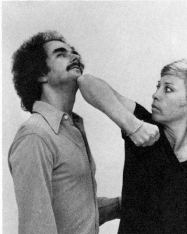

Elbow strike to chin

Chop to throat

23

Side-of-fist strike to jaw

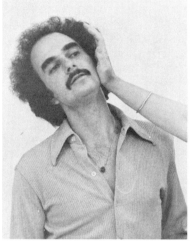

Palm-heel strike to jaw

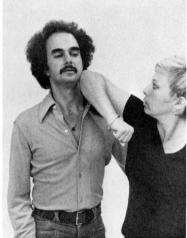

Elbow strike to jaw

Chop to jaw

Elbow strike to solar plexus

Grabbing finger and forcing back

Kick to groin

Knee to groin

Side-of-fist strike to groin

Side kick to knee

Kicking and scraping shin with foot

Stomping on foot

4.

WARM-UP EXERCISES

Always begin a practice session with warm-up exercises. They will help you achieve maximum agility, strength, and flexibility. The exercises included in this book are beneficial in preparing for the movements required in self-defense techniques. They are divided into three categories: Group I, total-body exercises and practice of basic techniques; Group II, strengthening exercises; and Group III, stretching exercises. You may select from among those suggested here, or you may substitute others that serve the same purposes.

You don't have to perform all the warm-up exercises listed each time you practice, but do include some from each group. Practice of the basic techniques (Group I), once all have been learned, should consist of: five front kicks, each leg; five side kicks, each leg; five back kicks, each leg; five palm-heel strikes, each arm; five side-of-fist strikes, each arm; five elbow strikes, each arm; and five blocks, each arm.

GROUP I

JOGGING

Jog in place or around the room for some thirty seconds at first, gradually building up to two minutes each exercise session.

JUMPING ROPE

Jump rope for one to three minutes; alternate hopping on both feet simultaneously with one-foot hopping for balance.

JUMPING JACKS

Start with ten jumping jacks and gradually build up to thirty or more each exercise session.

SHIFTING WEIGHT

Practice slide stepping to each side and forward and back.

CHANGING DIRECTION

Practice leaping from one foot to the other in all directions and practice a dodging motion with upper part of body.

DOWN AND OUT

Squat down and put hands on floor by feet. Jump feet back to a toe-pushup position. Jump feet forward between hands and stand.

KICKS

Practice each basic kick ten times with each leg. Shout with each kick. Practice to build accuracy first, speed second.

STRIKES

Practice each strike ten times with each arm. Shout with each strike. Practice to build accuracy first, speed second.

GROUP II

SITUPS

Bend your knees. Touch both elbows to both knees and bring elbows all the way back down to floor.

HOLDUPS

Hold body in toe-pushup position. Count to ten. Lower body to floor and relax.

PUSHUPS

Push body up in a straight line from knees. Bend arms to lower body in a straight line to a level below elbows. Push up again.

LEG LIFTS

Lift leg forward and back, then across in front and out to side, so that leg is lifted in all directions. Work on balance during this exercise.

SCISSORS KICKS

Sit with legs out and lean back on elbows. Lift both legs and alternate crossing them over and under each other.

PRONE ARCH

Lie face down, hands at side. Lift upper part of body, arms, and legs and hold for count of ten. Lower slowly.

TUCK AND ROLL

Lie on back in T position, arms outstretched. Tuck knees to chest and roll to touch knees to floor on one side, then the other. Keep knees tucked as tightly as possible.

ARM CIRCLES

Stand with arms outstretched. Rotate arms forward in four big circles, then fast in eight small circles. Repeat in backward circles.

GROUP III

STATIC HANG

Stand and bend down from waist. Lean weight onto balls of feet. Try to hold for thirty seconds.

CROSS-LEG STRETCH

Cross one leg over the other and lean down to touch floor. Alternate legs.

HIGH KICKS

Kick high in front with one hand extended as target, then high in back.

BACK STRETCH

Lie flat on back. Bend knees to chest, roll back, extend legs, and touch toes to floor behind head. Roll forward in reverse order to starting position.

TORSO TWIST

Stand with arms outstretched. Pivot upper part of body to move arms around to left, then around to right.

SIT AND REACH

Sit with legs apart. Grasp one leg with both hands as far down as you can reach. Bend elbows to bring upper part of body closer to leg. Alternate legs.

SIDE STRETCH

Sit with legs apart. Grasp right ankle with right hand. Stretch left arm over head and lower body to right leg. Alternate sides.

HURDLE

Sit with one leg outstretched, other leg bent back at knee. Grasp straight leg and bend elbows to press upper part of body to leg. Alternate sides. Increase angle between legs each time the exercise is done.

part two

TECHNIQUES OF SELF-DEFENSE

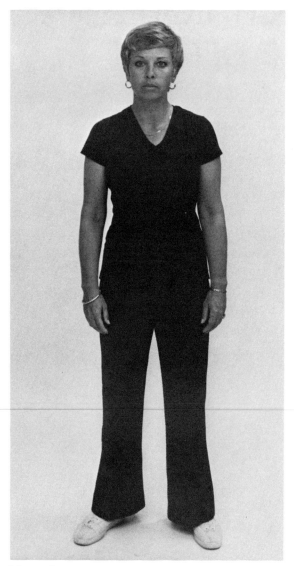

Natural stance

Fighting stance

5

THE FIGHTING STANCE

The fighting stance is useful for achieving maximum balance, agility, and speed. From the fighting stance you can move quickly in any direction, and it is the base from which you should learn most of the self-defense techniques. It is helpful to adopt this position in an attack situation, but if you are attacked without warning, concentrate more on balance than on stance. You can fight from any position as long as you maintain balance.

To move into the fighting stance, first assume a natural stance: body facing forward, feet slightly apart, arms hanging at side. Then—

1. Step right foot back and out to the side at a forty-five degree angle. Place feet shoulder width apart, knees slightly bent. Rotate hips a quarter turn to the right.

2. Bend left arm in front of you, elbow low, with fist raised to shoulder level, palm facing toward you.

3. Pull right hand back to hip, elbow pointing back and fist held close in to waist with palm facing up.

Don't tense up. Relax muscles so your body can react quickly.

This stance is usually best for strikes, kicks, and other movements with the right arm and leg. For movements using the left arm and leg, reverse the instructions above: left foot back, hips to the left, right arm in front, left elbow pointing back, left fist at side. When learning the following techniques, practice with both left and right arms and legs.

6.

USE OF ARMS, ELBOWS, AND HANDS

As the techniques outlined in this chapter demonstrate, you have powerful weapons in your arms and hands. Because arms are not as strong as legs, however, it is always best in an attack situation to keep your assailant more than arm's reach away. If the option is yours, keep the attacker at a distance by moving yourself out of his hitting range and by using your legs to kick him. Keep in mind that your legs are longer than his arms.

You may not have a choice. An attacker often strikes without warning or grabs before you have a chance for evasion. If he manages to get in close, all is not lost. The following strikes and chops can be used to gain control, the blocks to prevent pain. Don't hesitate to use them if an attacker gets within arm's range. But remember: If you can reach him, he can reach you. So practice striking quickly, accurately, and with force.

Dodge whenever you can; block whenever you can't.

Blocks should be considered last-resort measures to avoid getting hurt. If you can move out of the way of a blow, don't stand there and attempt to block it instead. Blocking requires a lot of practice and quick reflexes. Don't expect to be able to hold off an attacker with the block alone; follow through immediately with a counterattack of strikes and kicks. When practicing blocks with a partner, take it easy and use protective equipment.

The self-defense moves described in this book are broken down into their component steps. When learning a new move, practice it slowly, one step at a time, concentrating on accuracy and form. Once you've learned the move and proper form, gradually increase speed until the steps blend together into one fast, accurate, fluid movement.

Following many of the moves are lists of "do's" and "don't's" that point out common mistakes and how to avoid them.

In executing all strikes, chops, and blocks, remember:

1. *Accuracy*—for maximum effectiveness, hit on target.

2. *Speed*—strike quickly and snap back so you can strike again.

3. *Power*—keep arm muscles tight when striking and blocking, and *shout on impact.*

1. Assume fighting stance. Whenever possible, have opposite leg forward for palm-heel strike.

2. Open palm. Turn hand to striking position.

TARGET AREAS

  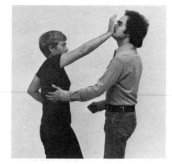

Nose Chin   Mouth

3. Thrust shoulder toward opponent. Pull other hand back.

4. Make contact with palm heel. Keep elbow slightly bent. Snap back so you can strike again.

DON'T lean forward while striking.

DON'T hit with arm only.

DON'T close fist.

DON'T lock elbow.

DON'T hit in a circular motion.

DON'T leave nonstriking hand out.

DO keep weight evenly distributed on both feet.

DO use shoulders and hips to drive arm forward.

DO keep hand open.

DO keep elbow slightly bent.

DO hit straight in.

DO pull it back as a counterforce.

NOTES: Be careful not to lock your elbow. Leave it slightly bent to cushion the force of the blow and prevent injury to your arm. When hitting against a pad in practice, don't make contact with your fingers. Keep your hand cocked back and make contact with the heel of the palm. If you make contact with another part of the hand, you risk a wrist sprain.

SIDE-OF-FIST STRIKE: HITTING DOWN

1. Lift fist high.

2. Come down hard on target.

TARGET AREA

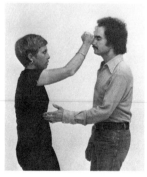

Nose

3. Drive through.

DON'T keep thumb inside fist.	DO keep thumb outside and folded down.
DON'T lock elbow.	DO keep elbow slightly bent.
DON'T use inside of fist (thumb side).	DO hit with outside of fist (little-finger side).
DON'T use only arm when striking.	DO use whole body to drive fist.
DON'T wind up too far.	DO use a short windup; it takes less time and does not telegraph your intentions.
DON'T delay.	DO use speed with this move, since it is relatively easy to block.

SIDE-OF-FIST STRIKE: HITTING FROM SIDE

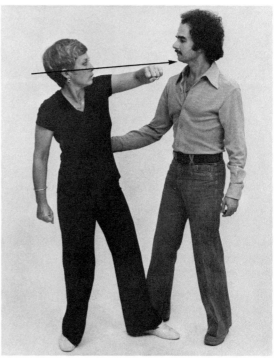

1. Lift fist up and to side.

2. Swing body to drive arm.

TARGET AREA

Chin

Side of face

Temple

Ear

Mouth

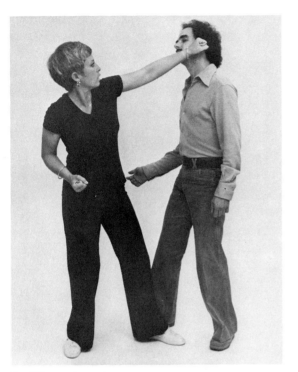

3. Hit on target.

DON'T keep thumb inside fist.	DO keep thumb outside and folded down.
DON'T lock elbow.	DO keep elbow slightly bent.
DON'T use inside of fist (thumb side).	DO hit with outside of fist (little-finger side).
DON'T use only arm when striking.	DO use whole body to drive fist.
DON'T wind up too far.	DO use a short windup; it takes less time and does not telegraph your intentions.
DON'T delay.	DO use speed with this move, since it is relatively easy to block.

SIDE-OF-FIST STRIKE: HITTING BACK

1. Lift fist high.

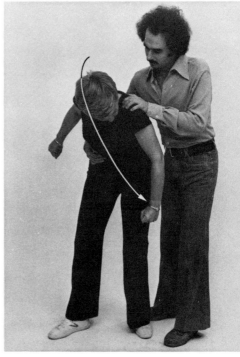

2. Swing fist down and back.

TARGET AREA

Groin

3. Strike target.

DON'T keep thumb inside fist.	DO keep thumb outside and folded down.
DON'T lock elbow.	DO keep elbow slightly bent.
DON'T use inside of fist (thumb side).	DO hit with outside of fist (little-finger side).
DON'T use only arm when striking.	DO use whole body to drive fist.
DON'T wind up too far.	DO use a short windup; it takes less time and does not telegraph your intentions.
DON'T delay.	DO use speed with this move, since it is relatively easy to block.

1. Raise hand to level of head close to ear. Have elbow high and keep fingers, including thumb, tightly together.

2. Move elbow first to throw hand with force.

TARGET AREAS

 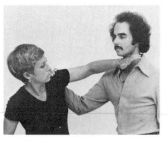 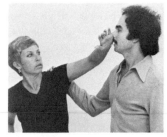

Side of face

Throat

Underneath nose

Top of nose

Temple

Side of neck

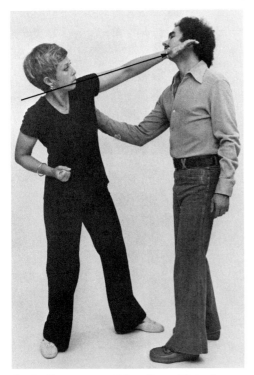

3. Strike target with edge of hand.

DON'T spread fingers.   DO keep fingers tightly together.
DON'T lock elbow.   DO keep elbow slightly bent.
DON'T hit with fingers.   DO make contact with side of hand.

ELBOW STRIKE: FORWARD

1. Make fist. Lift elbow high. Keep forearm in line with upper arm.

2. Pivot body and thrust forearm forward. Contact with forearm just below elbow.

TARGET AREA

Face

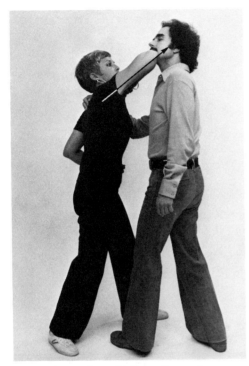

3. Strike to face. Follow through.

ELBOW STRIKE: BACKWARD-DOWN

1. Lift fist high.

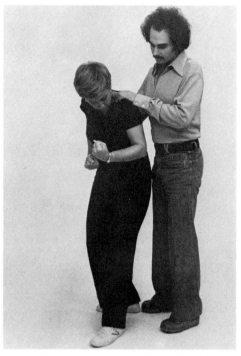

2. Look at target area. Pivot body and thrust elbow down and back, hard. Keep elbow close to body.

TARGET AREA

Solar plexus

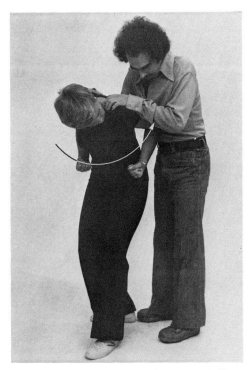

3. Strike to solar plexus. Follow
   through.

ELBOW STRIKE: BACKWARD-UP

1. Lift fist shoulder high.

2. Look at target area. Pivot body and thrust elbow up and back.

TARGET AREAS

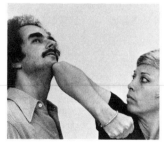 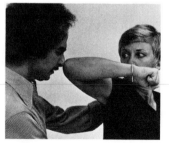 

Chin

Nose

Jaw

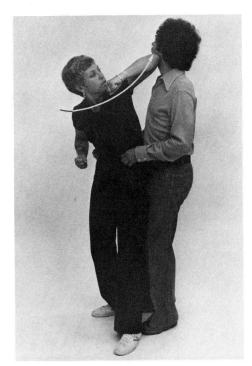

3. Strike to target area. Follow through.

1. Make fist and raise forearm. Keep elbow bent. Keep forearm horizontal.

2. Keep hand about six inches out from head, while rotating opposite hip away from block.

3. Pull opposite hand back and prepare
   to strike.

DON'T block your vision.   DO raise arm high.
DON'T drop elbow.   DO keep forearm horizontal.
DON'T relax arm.   DO keep muscles tight.

NOTES: Try to move quickly to avoid an attacker's blow. If you cannot avoid the blow, block and follow through with a counterattack.

Whenever possible, have foot forward on the same side as the blocking arm: left foot forward for block with the left arm, right foot forward for right-arm block.

Take it easy in practice; a block can hurt. Use pads or batakas if possible.

1. Make fist and raise it with elbow bent. Keep forearm vertical.

2. Bring forearm across and in front of chest, rotating hips in direction of block. Keep forearm vertical and below chin.

3. Pull opposite hand back and prepare
   to strike.

DON'T lift elbow.
DON'T allow fist to block vision.
DON'T open hand.
DON'T block halfway.

DO keep forearm vertical.
DO keep fist below eye level.
DO keep fist and arms tight.
DO make big sweeping move-
   ment and follow through.

NOTES: Take it easy in practice. A block can hurt. Use pads or batakas if possible.

 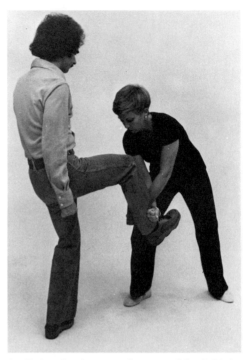

1. Make two fists and cross one forearm over the other. Keep fists wide apart.

2. Bring both arms down to block kick. Bend knees and put weight on front foot.

3. If possible, grab attacker's foot and lift as follow-up. Counter with kick or strike.

DON'T open hands. DO keep fists tight.
DON'T bend too far forward. DO bend knees, not back.

NOTES: Take it easy in practice. A block can hurt. Use pads or batakas if possible.

7.

USE OF LEGS, KNEES, AND FEET

Never stand still for an attacker (unless he has a weapon) if you can move about; a moving target is more difficult to hit or grab. Use your legs to play "keep away." If an attacker manages to move in, kick if you can to keep your head out of his reach. Remember, your legs are longer than his arms. Use them for power, agility, and balance.

When kicking, keep your supporting knee slightly bent to aid your balance and keep your supporting foot flat on the ground. Practice shifting weight and changing direction until you can move quickly and maintain your balance.

High kicks are not necessary and are not recommended. You will be more accurate with low kicks than with high kicks. You do not need to kick above the man's groin level to disable him. Your target areas are the groin, the knee, and the shin. Trying to kick higher—at his face, for example—only reduces your chances of maintaining balance and of hitting accurately. You don't need a lot of fancy legwork, just a few simple, effective moves.

Practice judging distance for kicking. If your opponent is in too close, a kick may not be as effective as a strike. You need enough distance to extend your leg at least three-quarters of the way to get enough power behind the kick. If he is too close for a kick, use your hands or elbows, stomp on his foot, or jab your knee into his groin.

Be careful of your toes; they are fragile. If you practice without shoes on, remember not to make contact with your toes, even when kicking against a pad. Make contact with the bottom of your foot—either the ball of the foot or the heel, depending on the kind of kick.

In all kicks, remember:

1. *Accuracy*—for maximum effectiveness, you must hit on target.

2. *Speed*—kick as fast as you can and snap back so you can kick again and again.

3. *Power*—use your torso muscles too when throwing kicks and strikes; put your whole body into every blow and *shout on impact*.

1. Start (and end) with fighting stance.

2. Lift knee high, keeping supporting knee slightly bent.

TARGET AREAS

Groin   Knee   Shin

3. Snap leg forward from the knee. Make contact with ball of foot. Shout on impact.

4. Pull foot back quickly, keeping knee high. Resume stance.

DON'T lift heel of supporting foot off floor.	DO keep supporting foot flat.
DON'T drop knee after kick.	DO snap back before stepping down.
DON'T try to kick with heel.	DO use ball of foot.
DON'T take your eyes off target.	DO focus on target of kick.
DON'T drop hands while kicking.	DO keep hands up for protection.
DON'T straighten supporting leg.	DO keep supporting knee bent.
DON'T kick too high.	DO keep all kicks below waist.

NOTES: Practice steps 2, 3, and 4 in separate movements: lift, snap, pull back, then step down. The movements will become more fluid as you gain speed, but be sure not to kick out before the knee is raised.

When you are not wearing shoes, contact should be made with the ball of your foot to avoid injury to your toes.

Speed is important, not only for power but also for safety. If you kick too slowly, your opponent may catch your foot.

1. Start with front fighting stance and pivot to side, with kicking leg nearest opponent.

2. Lift knee high, keeping supporting knee bent.

TARGET AREAS

Knee   Groin

3. Leaning slightly away from kick, drive foot out to side. Contact with flat of heel. Shout on impact.

4. Snap foot back quickly, keeping knee high. Resume stance.

DON'T look away from target.

DON'T side kick when facing opponent.

DON'T turn your back to opponent.

DON'T kick with supporting foot toward opponent.

DON'T kick with your toes.

DON'T kick halfway.

DON'T kick up.

DON'T straighten supporting leg.

DON'T kick slowly.

DON'T leave kicking leg extended.

DON'T lower arms when kicking.

DO focus on target; accuracy is important.

DO kick with your side to him.

DO turn only enough to have your side to him.

DO pivot supporting foot away from opponent.

DO contact with flat of heel.

DO drive your foot *through* target.

DO lift knee high and kick down and out.

DO keep supporting knee bent.

DO kick quickly; speed is power.

DO snap back quickly to a bent-knee position.

DO keep arms up for protection.

NOTES: Don't bend your ankle when executing a side kick; the bone may break.

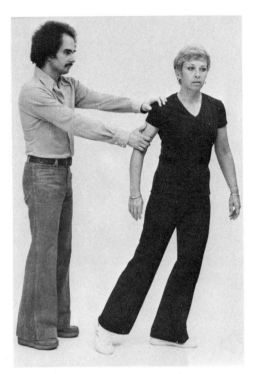

1. Rear attack may not give you a chance to assume fighting stance.

2. Lift knee, keeping supporting knee bent. Turn your head to look at target.

TARGET AREAS

Knee

Groin

3. Kick backward with flat of foot. Shout on impact.

4. Snap knee forward quickly.

DON'T kick without looking.

DON'T straighten leg.

DON'T raise knee too far.

DON'T leave your foot out after kicking.

DON'T kick too high.

DON'T lean too far away from attacker.

DON'T kick with your toes pointed.

DO look at target.

DO keep supporting knee bent.

DO kick quickly.

DO snap knee forward again quickly.

DO keep all kicks below attacker's waist.

DO keep your balance.

DO contact with flat of foot, preferably heel.

1. Lift knee high, keeping supporting knee bent.

2. Look at target. Stomp down hard with heel.

TARGET AREAS

Instep

Toes

DON'T look away from target.   DO focus on target.

NOTES: When practicing on a hard surface, don't stomp with full force; you may injure your foot.

    Don't rely on a stomp alone to disable an attacker. Follow through with a disabling move.

1. Attacker is in close.

2. Lift knee sharply into groin.

3. Attacker is bent down.

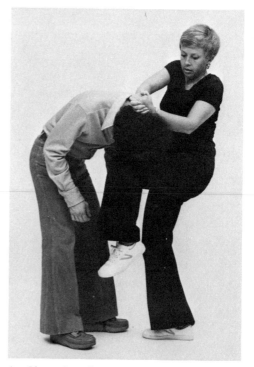

4. Clasp hands together and use side-of-fist strike to back of head, or pull on ears or hair to pull head down; then lift knee sharply to face.

part three

APPLYING SELF-DEFENSE IN ATTACK SITUATIONS

8

INTRODUCTION

In this section, we will show how the self-defense techniques —strikes, chops, blocks, stomps, kicks—can be applied to specific attack situations. We have not included all the possible defenses for each attack situation, nor could we include every possible kind of attack. If you find yourself in a situation you have not studied, improvise. Something you have learned will probably apply. If you hear of another defense for a situation, and you think it will work better for you, use it. There are no set rules to restrict you. Remain flexible and make your defense fit the situation.

Keep in mind that the most effective defense is avoiding physical contact whenever possible. Try to find another way out of a dangerous situation. You may still get hurt even if you put up a fight, so don't decide you can handle any situation with physical combat. An attacker with a weapon is especially dangerous, and in such a situation physical combat should be avoided by any means possible. If you are forced to use physical tactics to defend yourself, be willing to act. Don't hold back; try not to let pain break your defense. Absorb any temporary pain in order to prevent a more permanent injury. More quickly, completing your defense and counterattack, and keep moving until you are safe.

Again, we suggest learning these techniques in the order they are presented in the schedule of lessons in Appendix 1. Learn each one thoroughly, review them in later lessons, and when you've learned them all, review them regularly as part of an ongoing fitness and self-defense program so you don't get rusty.

Above all, *practice these releases and counterattack moves until they become reflex actions.*

Following many of the moves are lists of "do's" and "don't's" that point out common mistakes and how to avoid them.

DEFENSE AGAINST GRABS AND CHOKES

Chokes and grabs are common forms of attack against women. Even when being choked, however, you are not at the greatest disadvantage: The man is committed to a certain position momentarily, and his hands are busy, so his vulnerable areas are open to your strikes and kicks. Move quickly and with accuracy and force. Once you get past the initial shock of actually being attacked, turn the element of surprise to work for you. He doesn't expect you to resist effectively.

A few throws are included here. Throws are difficult to perform and require advanced skill. If you expect to rely on a throw, practice until your moves are quick and automatic.

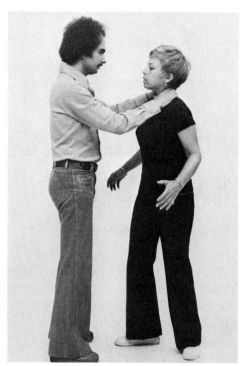

1. Attacker chokes.

2. Lift both arms straight up close to ears.

DON'T bend arms when pivoting in release.

DON'T keep feet together.

DO lift both arms straight up.

DO take a step if necessary to maintain balance.

3. Pivot sharply—arms, torso, hips. Thrust shoulder across attacker's wrists.

4. Pivot back quickly in a counterattack.

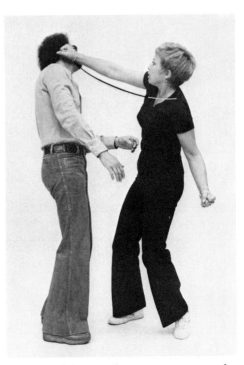

5. Side-of-fist strike to ear, temple, jaw, or nose. Shout on impact.

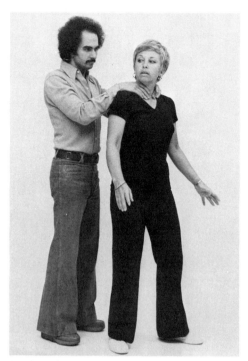

1. Attacker chokes from behind.

2. Lift both arms straight up close to ears.

DON'T bend arms when pivoting in release.

DON'T keep feet together.

DO lift both arms straight up.

DO take a step if necessary to maintain balance.

3. Pivot sharply. Thrust shoulder across attacker's wrists.

4. Continue turning in a counterattack.

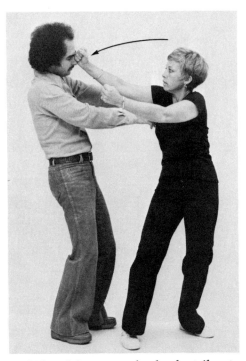

5. Side-of-fist or palm-heel strike to ear, temple, jaw, or nose. Shout on impact.

1. Attacker grabs from behind. (Most attackers will use right arm, but practice both sides.)

2. Tuck chin in tight. Lift up inside hand (left hand for right-arm choke).

DON'T lift up chin and pull against choke.	DO tuck chin in tight to relieve pressure.
DON'T pivot into your opponent.	DO pivot away from opponent's grasp.
DON'T hesitate.	DO move quickly and use element of surprise.
DON'T attempt release before inflicting pain to distract him.	DO use strike or stomp to distract him briefly.
DON'T pivot without moving feet for balance.	DO step out with one foot to maintain balance.
DON'T hesitate following release.	DO counterattack immediately to disable attacker.

3. Make fist and execute elbow strike to stomach or side-of-fist strike to groin. Stomp on attacker's foot.

4. Pivot away from attacker (for right-arm choke bring left side forward and step out with left foot).

5. Counterattack with strikes to face or kicks, depending on distance. Shout on impact.

REAR CHOKE WITH ARMS: SHOULDER THROW FOR ADVANCED STUDENTS

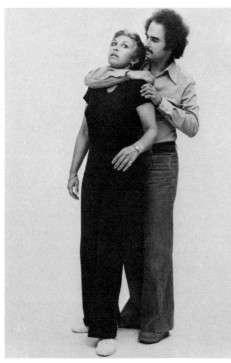

1. Attacker grabs from behind.

2. Grab wrist and elbow of choking arm and hold tight.

. Drop lower by bending knees and waist, and step forward with right foot.

4. Pivot shoulders sharply counter-clockwise and turn head to look over left shoulder, pushing up with left leg to throw attacker off balance. Counterattack with appropriate moves.

DON'T bend only at knees.

DON'T look down when you pivot.

DON'T try to lift attacker.

DON'T bend down too far (you don't want attacker to fall on you).

DO bend knees and waist and step forward.

DO turn head sharply to look over left shoulder.

DO roll attacker over your lower shoulder.

DO bend only enough to throw attacker off balance.

NOTES: Throws are difficult to perform successfully and require advanced skill. Practice until your moves are quick and automatic.

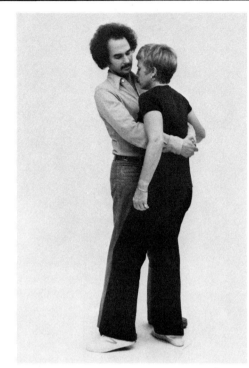 

1. Attacker grabs; your arms are free.

2. Lift strong arm high. Pull attacker's hair back from hairline with other hand.

3. Strike down hard with side of fist to bridge of nose . . .

4. *or* palm-heel strike to throat, chin, or nose . . .

5. *or* pop both ears by hitting hard with cupped hands . . .

6. *or* knee kick to groin or stomp on foot.

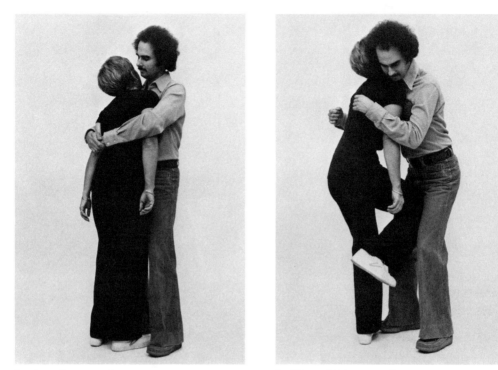

1. Attacker grabs; your arms are trapped.

2. Knee kick to groin . . .

3. *or* stomp on foot . . .

4. *or* bite hard at neck or shoulder . . .

5. *or* if close enough, strike attacker's nose with your forehead.

6. Counterattack, following release, with palm-heel strike.

REAR UNDERARM BEAR HUG

1. Attacker grabs; your arms are free.

2. Move hips to one side. Side-of-fist strike to groin . . .

REAR OVERARM BEAR HUG

1. Attacker grabs; your arms are trapped.

2. Move hips to one side. Side-of-fist strike to groin.

3. *or* elbow strike to face . . .

4. *or* stomp on foot. Use appropriate counterattack to disable assailant.

3. Lift knee high and stomp on foot.

4. Butt head back to nose.

REAR OVERARM BEAR HUG: HIP THROW FOR ADVANCED STUDENTS

1. Attacker grabs from behind.

2. Move your hips quickly to one side. Step out to the side with outside foot.

3. Lift inside foot and place it behind attacker.

4. Pivot around inside leg to throw attacker off balance backward. Counterattack immediately with appropriate moves.

DON'T attempt to throw attacker by merely straightening up your body.

DON'T hesitate.

DO pivot sharply around.

DO move quickly and use element of surprise; counterattack immediately.

NOTES: Throws are difficult to perform successfully and require advanced skill. Practice until your moves are quick and automatic.

1. Attacker grabs wrist.

2. Open your fist and press your elbow toward attacker.

3. Yank wrist from between attacker's thumb and forefinger (weakest part of his grip).

4. Raise fist high.

5. Counterattack with side-of-fist strike or palm-heel strike or kick.

WRIST GRAB WITH ONE HAND: ALTERNATE

1. Attacker grabs wrist.

2. Lift knee high.

3. Side kick to attacker's knee . . .

4. *or* front kick to groin.

DON'T pull against palm to release.	DO pull through thumb and forefinger opening.
DON'T hesitate.	DO move quickly and use element of surprise.
DON'T give up if release is delayed.	DO continue kicking and striking.

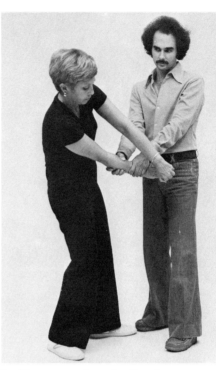

1. Attacker grabs wrist.

2. Open your hands. Reach across over the top with your free hand and grab your trapped hand.

3. Swing arms in a big circle, moving up, over, and down.

4. Counterattack with side-of-fist or palm-heel strike or kick.

DON'T reach under to grab your own hand.

DON'T attempt to pull out of grip.

DON'T hesitate before or after release.

DO always reach over attacker's arms.

DO make a big circular movement with both arms.

DO move quickly and counterattack to disable attacker.

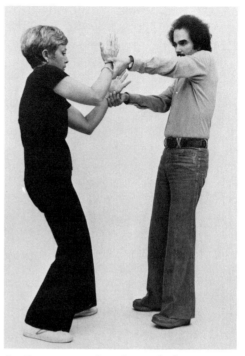

1. Attacker grabs both wrists.

2. Open your hands and thrust your bent elbows toward attacker.

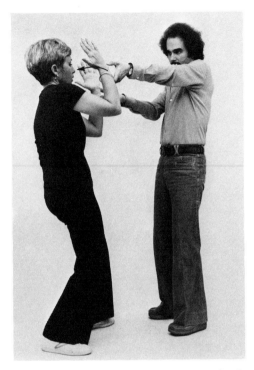

3. Yank wrists from between attacker's thumbs and forefingers.

4. Counterattack with kick or palm-heel strike or knee to groin.

DON'T attempt to pull loose.

DON'T hesitate before or after release.

DO bend elbows and yank wrists upward.

DO move quickly and counterattack to disable attacker.

BOTH WRISTS GRABBED FROM BEHIND

 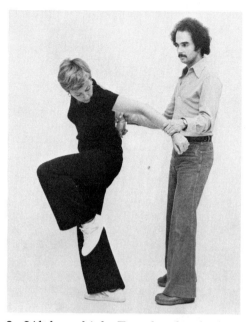

1. Attacker grabs both wrists from behind.

2. Lift knee high. Turn head to look at target.

BOTH ARMS GRABBED FROM BEHIND

1. Attacker grabs both arms from behind.

2. Lift knee high. Look down at target.

3. Back kick to attacker's knee.

4. Counterattack with more kicks or palm-heel strike.

3. Stomp on foot hard.

4. Butt head back to chin or nose.

1. Attacker grabs arm from side.

2. Pivot and raise knee.

ARM GRAB: REAR THROW FOR ADVANCED STUDENTS

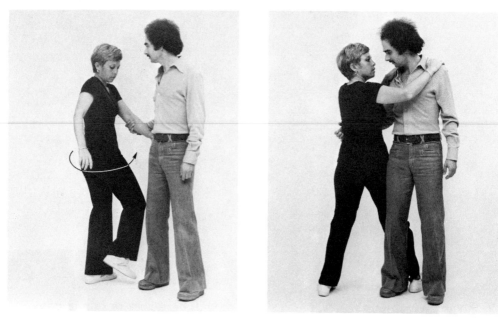

1. Attacker grabs arm; pivot.

2. Place one foot behind attacker.

3. Side kick to attacker's knee.

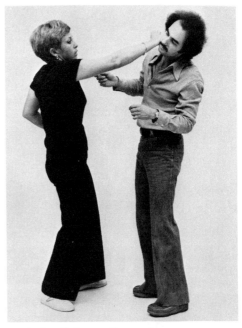

4. Side-of-fist strike to face.

3. Push attacker over your foot.

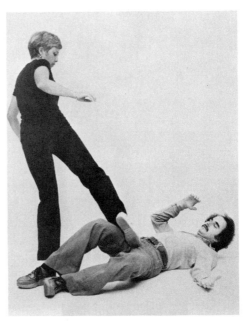

4. Kick.

 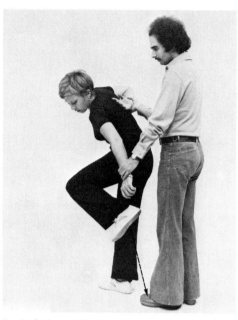

1. Attacker grabs arms.

2. Lift knee high. Stomp hard on attacker's foot.

HEAD LOCK

1. Attacker locks your head under his arm.

2. Push thumb into back of attacker's knee. Grab attacker's hair with other hand.

3. Elbow strike to side of face.

4. Pivot, step away, and kick.

3. Push on leg and yank back and down on hair.

4. Counterattack with kick to groin.

103

1. Attacker grabs.

2. Stomp on attacker's foot.

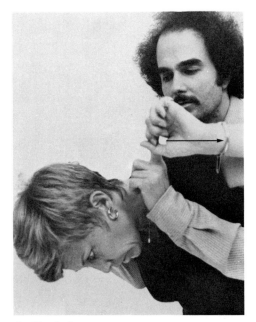

3. Reach behind and grab attacker's fingers.

4. Yank fingers.

5. Counterattack with elbow strike or other disabling move.

CLOTHES GRAB

1. Attacker grabs lapel or blouse.

2. Lift fist of stronger arm high.

HAIR GRAB

1. Attacker grabs hair.

2. Grab his hand with both your hands. Press against scalp.

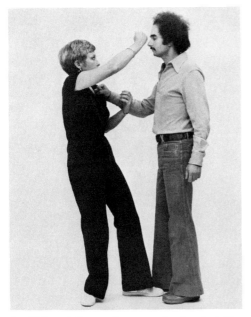

3. Side-of-fist strike or palm-heel strike to nose or chin.

4. Knee kick to groin.

3. Pivot body.

4. Side kick to knee.

MOUTH AND WAIST GRAB

1. Attacker grabs from behind.

2. Lift knee high. Stomp on attacker's foot.

3. Lift fist high; move hips to one side.

4. Side-of-fist strike to groin.

5. Elbow strike to face.

FORCED WALK: TRIP FOR ADVANCED STUDENTS

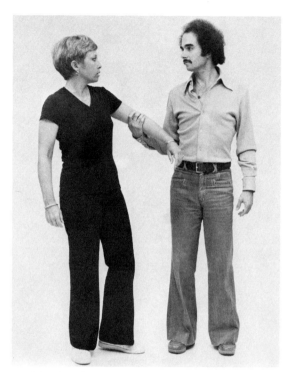

1. Attacker holds you in close by your upper arm and forces you to accompany him.

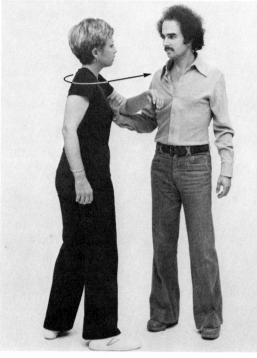

2. Let him think you're going along with him. Say "okay" and go a couple of steps with him. Still talking, turn to face him and, while he's thinking about what you're saying, step out to the side with one foot.

3. Step quickly behind him with other foot.

4. Place hand on attacker's shoulder. Use foot that is behind attacker to sweep his foot off floor. Push back and down on his shoulder to throw him off balance over your leg. Counterattack with disabling moves.

DON'T hesitate.

DO move quickly; throws require element of surprise to work; counterattack immediately.

1. Attacker attempts to force his way into your home.

2. Kick shin. Stomp on foot.

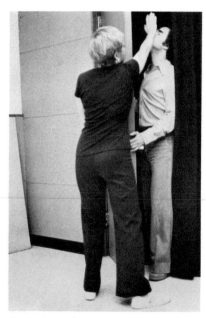

3. Palm-heel strike or side-of-fist strike to nose.

4. Slam and lock door. Telephone police.

10.
DEFENSE AGAINST NONVIOLENT ATTACKS

When your "attacker" is more of a nuisance than a threat, you don't need to throw him or disable him. Use less drastic measures to control him: a finger pull or a wrist lock should take care of unwelcome advances when your protests have no effect. Make your defense fit the situation.

UNWELCOME HAND ON KNEE

1. A man seated next to you won't remove his hand from your knee.

2. Grab one of his fingers with one hand and grab his wrist with the other hand.

UNWELCOME EMBRACE

1. A man puts his arm around you or moves in for an unwelcome kiss or hug.

2. Press palm heel under his nose and push.

3. Bend finger back.

3. Cup your hand and push with fingers and thumb into throat area under chin.

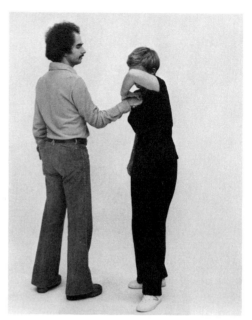

1. A person grabs your clothes, but poses no physical harm to you.

2. Lift elbow high. Reach over his arm. Grab his hand with your thumb on top.

NOTES: Be gentle when practicing with a partner; the wrist is fragile.

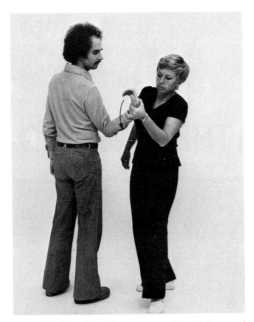

3. Jerk his hand out to the side and bend it back at wrist.

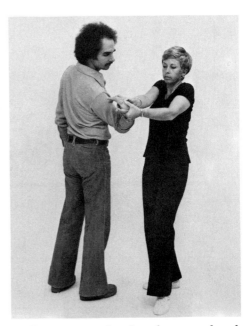

4. Bring your other hand over and grab his hand so that both your thumbs are on back of his hand.

5. Continue bending his hand back and out to the side.

11.

DEFENSE FROM THE GROUND

Although it is more difficult to escape when you are lying down than when you are upright, you do have a few slight advantages if attacked when you are on the ground or in bed. Your back is not exposed; you don't have to worry about maintaining balance; and you have some support behind your kicks and strikes. You can deliver powerful and damaging kicks from a downed position, and you can give a successful palm-heel strike or side-of-fist strike if the attacker is leaning over you.

The following defenses, when executed successfully, will enable you to get to your feet and then counterattack with a series of moves to disable your attacker.

APPROACH TOWARD THE GROUND

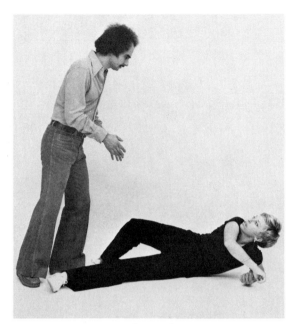

1. Attacker approaches when you are in a fallen position.

2. Tuck body tight by pulling knees toward chest. Defend head with stronger arm. Prop up on other elbow.

3. Deliver series of kicks to attacker's knee . . .

4. *or* kicks to groin.

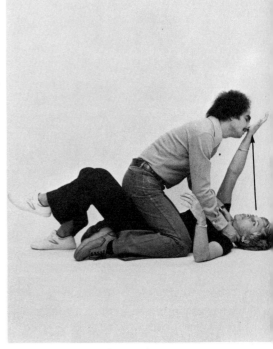

1. Attacker straddles you and chokes or holds you.

2. Palm-heel strike to chin or nose over attacker's arms.

Push hard with one leg and try to roll over to get attacker's weight off you.

4. Get to your feet if you can. Counterattack with kicks or palm-heel strikes whether or not you are standing.

NOTES: A strong palm-heel strike will probably surprise an attacker as well as cause him pain. That moment of surprise is your best chance to try to get to your feet.

1. Attacker pins you to floor and leans head down toward you.

2. Jerk your head up quickly and hit his nose with your forehead.

3. Palm-heel strike to chin or nose. Roll away, get up, kick.

12

DEFENSE AGAINST STRIKING AND KICKING ATTACKS

Striking and kicking attacks are not the most common forms of attack against women, but you may be confronted by them at some time. Move out of your assailant's reach if possible. If not, block and counterattack immediately. Remember that most men are stronger than most women, so use the block only as a last resort.

1. Attacker shoves with one hand.

2. Grab his wrist from underneath with your palm up.

DON'T delay gripping his wrist and hand.	DO place both your hands simultaneously.
DON'T bend with your knees.	DO bend at waist and press upper part of your body against his hand as his wrist bends backward.
DON'T hold lightly.	DO grab and press hard.
DON'T grab with your palm facing down.	DO grab with palm facing up.

NOTES: When practicing, take it easy. Your partner must bend down with you to avoid injury to his wrist. If your partner delays or resists, his wrist may be injured.

3. Simultaneously place your other hand flat against his hand and press tight to your own body.

4. Bend forward at waist and step back with one foot, pulling him toward you.

5. Jab your knee into his face.

1. Attacker slaps.

2. Move to dodge slap, if possible. If not, step back and block with outside arm.

Counterattack with palm-heel strike
to nose or chin . . .

4. *or* front kick or knee to groin.

DON'T stand still and depend on block alone.

DON'T block with open hand.

DON'T give half-hearted block.

DON'T delay following block.
DON'T deliver palm-heel strike with arm only.

DO, if possible, move out of reach of slap and avoid having to block it.

DO make tight fist to tighten arm muscles.

DO move quickly, with force, and shout.

DO counterattack immediately.

DO pivot body to throw palm-heel strike.

1. Attacker kicks.

2. Move to dodge kick, if possible.

3. Use low block by crossing your arms at the wrists and catching kick with bottom of the X.

4. Grab his foot and pull hard. Counterattack with appropriate moves.

DON'T block with open hand.

DO always block with fists tight; with this block, any extended fingers may be injured.

DON'T extend arms separately.
DON'T delay before or after block.

DO keep wrists tightly together.
DO move quickly, with force; shout and counterattack.

1. Attacker throws punch to face. If possible, step back into fighting stance.

2. Lift forearm and block. Pull opposite hand back.

3. Counterattack with palm-heel strike to nose or chin . . .

4. *or* front kick to groin.

DON'T stand still and depend on block alone.	DO, if possible, move out of reach of punch and avoid having to block it.
DON'T block with open hand.	DO make tight fist to tighten arm muscles.
DON'T give half-hearted block.	DO move quickly, with force, and shout.
DON'T delay following block.	DO counterattack immediately.
DON'T deliver palm-heel strike with arm only.	DO pivot body to throw palm-heel strike.

NOTES: You will usually be better off if you move quickly to dodge the blow rather than meet it with a block. Maintain your distance from your attacker; make the moment of contact *your* option.

13.

DEFENSE AGAINST WEAPONS

Having to defend against a weapon attack is feared even by the experts. Defense against a weapon requires greater caution than any other attack situation. You must practice and develop advanced skills to hope for success against an armed assailant. Still, there may come a time when you have to choose between attempting such a defense and suffering passively. Try to avoid such an occurrence by any means possible.

ATTACK WITH BLUNT WEAPON FROM ABOVE

1. Attacker uses clubbing motion.

2. Use forceful upward block. Don't try to hold attacker's arm.

3. Counterattack immediately with palm-heel strike to nose or chin.

4. Knee or kick to groin.

1. Attacker approaches with knife in high position.

2. Step quickly to side away from knife. Use high block.

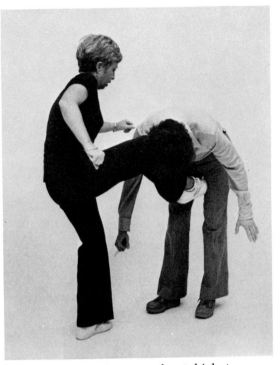

3. Palm-heel strike to nose or chin, if within range.

4. Side kick to knee or front kick to groin.

DON'T show panic.

DO try to remain cool and talk your way out whenever possible.

DON'T step too far away.
DON'T drop arms when kicking.

DO make your kicks count.
DO keep arms up to protect head and torso.

NOTES: *Never* attempt to grab the knife while the attacker is holding it. Block his forearm.

1. Attacker approaches with knife in middle position.

2. Step quickly to side away from knife. Lift knee for kick.

3. Side kick to knee.

4. Palm-heel strike to chin or nose.

DON'T show panic.	DO try to remain cool and talk your way out whenever possible.
DON'T step too far away.	DO make your kicks count.
DON'T drop arms when kicking.	DO keep arms up to protect head and torso.

NOTES: *Never* attempt to grab the knife while the attacker is holding it. Dodge to the side and kick.

1. Attacker approaches with knife in low position.

2. Block with chop to forearm and step quickly to side away from knife.

3. Palm-heel strike to nose or chin, if within range.

4. Side kick to knee or front kick to groin.

DON'T show panic.

DO try to remain cool and talk your way out whenever possible.

DON'T step too far away.
DON'T drop arms when kicking.

DO make your kicks count.
DO keep arms up to protect head and torso.

NOTES: *Never* attempt to grab the knife while the attacker is holding it. Dodge away; block his arm.

1. Attacker holds knife against you.

2. Swing your forearm hard against his forearm and knock his arm out to side.

3. Palm-heel strike to nose or chin.

4. Front kick to groin.

DON'T try to hold his arm away.

DON'T delay your counterattack.

DO knock his arm away as hard as you can.

DO counterattack immediately to disable him.

NOTES: *Never* attempt to grab the knife while the attacker is holding it.

1. Attacker moves knife horizontally in slicing motion.

2. Leap back quickly out of range of knife.

3. Raise knee; side kick to attacker's knee.

4. Kick to head or groin if he is down.

DON'T step too far away for a kick.

DON'T ever grab for knife.

DO leap out of knife's range, but reach attacker's knee with a quick kick.

DO use your legs to maintain distance during your counterattack.

STRANGLED FROM BEHIND WITH ROPE

1. Attacker strangles with rope from behind.

2. Grab rope if possible. Drop down and back against attacker.

3. Roll away and stand, if possible. Kick to groin or palm-heel strike to nose, depending on distance.

4. Continue counterattack with kicks or strikes.

DON'T pull against rope.

DON'T delay your counterattack.

DO drop back and down quickly to unbalance attacker.

DO counterattack immediately.

APPENDIXES

SCHEDULE OF LESSONS

LESSON 1
DISCUSS: Common sense of self-defense, SAFE
WARM-UP: Select from Groups I, II, and III
NEW SKILLS: Stance, shout, front kick
WRITE: List five dangerous situations you might expect to encounter

LESSON 2
DISCUSS: Natural weapons
WARM-UP: Select from Groups I, II, and III
NEW SKILLS: Palm-heel strike, knee, front choke
REVIEW: Front kick

LESSON 3
DISCUSS: Target areas
WARM-UP: Select from Groups I, II, and III
NEW SKILLS: Side kick, side-of-fist strike, wrist release (two hands, front)
REVIEW: Front choke

LESSON 4
DISCUSS: Psychological aspects of defense
WARM-UP: Select from Groups I, II, and III
NEW SKILLS: Elbow Strike, back kick, rear choke (hands)
REVIEW: Front choke, wrist release

LESSON 5
DISCUSS: Safety at home
WARM-UP: Select from Groups I, II, and III
NEW SKILLS: Stomp, chop, front bear hugs
REVIEW: Front choke, rear choke

LESSON 6

DISCUSS: Safety when walking

WARM-UP: Select from Groups I, II, and III

NEW SKILLS: High block and counterattack, wrist release (one hand, front), slap, punch

REVIEW: Front bear hugs, rear choke

LESSON 7

DISCUSS: Safety when driving

WARM-UP: Select from Groups I, II, and III

NEW SKILLS: Middle block and counterattack, shove

REVIEW: Wrist releases

LESSON 8

DISCUSS: Safety on the telephone

WARM-UP: Select from Groups I, II, and III

NEW SKILLS: Both wrists grabbed from behind, arms grabbed from behind

REVIEW: Punch, slap

LESSON 9

DISCUSS: Safety in an elevator

WARM-UP: Select from Groups I, II, and III

NEW SKILLS: Rear bear hugs, hip throw (optional)

REVIEW: Wrists grabbed from behind, arms grabbed from behind

LESSON 10

DISCUSS: Reporting to authorities

WARM-UP: Select from Groups I, II, and III

NEW SKILLS: Rear choke (arms), head lock

REVIEW: Rear bear hugs, front bear hugs, hip throw (optional)

LESSON 11

DISCUSS: Simple objects as weapons

WARM-UP: Select from Groups I, II, and III

NEW SKILLS: Full nelson, shoulder throw (optional)

REVIEW: Rear choke (arms), head lock

LESSON 12

DISCUSS: Common questions and myths

WARM-UP: Select from Groups I, II, and III

NEW SKILLS: Arm lock, mouth and waist grab, hair grab

REVIEW: Full nelson, shoulder throw (optional), rear choke (arms)

LESSON 13
DISCUSS: Behavior in rape attacks
WARM-UP: Select from Groups I, II, and III
NEW SKILLS: Defense from the ground
REVIEW: Front choke, rear choke (hands)

LESSON 14
DISCUSS: Behavior in robbery
WARM-UP: Select from Groups I, II, and III
NEW SKILLS: Forced entry, clothes grab, low block and counterattack, defense against kick
REVIEW: Front bear hugs

LESSON 15
DISCUSS: Behavior in assault
WARM-UP: Select from Groups I, II, and III
NEW SKILLS: Arm grab (side or front), trip (optional), nonviolent attacks
REVIEW: Rear bear hugs

LESSON 16
DISCUSS: Dangerous situations drawn from personal experience or news media, and possible defenses
WARM-UP: Select from Groups I, II, and III
NEW SKILLS: Strangled with rope, attack with blunt weapon
REVIEW: Defense from the ground

LESSON 17
DISCUSS: Behavior against weapons
WARM-UP: Select from Groups I, II, and III
NEW SKILLS: Attacks with knife
REVIEW: Chokes, bear hugs

LESSON 18
Show film, *Nobody's Victim* (see "Self-Defense Aids"); *or* arrange guest lecture or visit with police officer; *or* review all skills by moving with partner through the following circuit:
    a. Front chokes
    b. Rear chokes
    c. Front bear hugs
    d. Rear bear hugs
    e. Any kind of grab
    f. Defense from ground
    g. Defense against weapons

LESSON 19

WRITTEN: Give the defenses that could be used in the five situations listed during the first lesson.

REVIEW: All skills using circuit outlined in Lesson 18; if possible, video-tape for immediate viewing and self-analysis.

LESSON 20

SELF-EXAMINATION: Demonstrate basic techniques for kicks, strikes, and (optional) throws. Demonstrate successful self-defense in four out of five attack situations: chokes and grabs, defense from ground, striking and kicking attacks, nonviolent attacks, weapon attacks.

FOR THE INSTRUCTOR

CLASSROOM ORGANIZATION

1. Arrange class in rows four deep, if possible. This allows the instructor to look down a row and analyze movements of several students at once. Keep rows even in number from front to back to facilitate pairing off for partner practice of releases and counterattacks.

2. Emphasize the importance of self-discipline and total concentration in practicing the movements. The student should think about using proper form in each movement and should focus on the target area.

3. Begin each session with warm-ups. Jogging and jumping rope are excellent total-body warm-up exercises for self-defense classes. Always include: total-body exercises; practice in basic techniques of kicking, striking, and blocking; and exercises for strengthening and stretching.

4. Count each basic move out loud. The instructor can direct practice of the basics by counting loudly, "one," and having the students follow with the required movement and a shout of "one." The instructor then counts "two" and the students follow with a movement and a shout of "two," and so on until each basic move has been performed ten times.

5. When teaching a basic move or a combination of defensive tactics, break the movement down into its component parts and count each part of the move as the students perform it. As skill progresses, the count can be shortened and the movement performed at faster tempo. Progress slowly so the students retain proper form while adding speed. When teaching a side kick, for example, the instructor can count:

One—lift knee and pivot slightly on supporting foot.
Two—extend foot out and down, and lean away from kick.
Three—bring foot back quickly with knee kept high and bent.
Four—resume balanced stance with both feet on floor.

153

Later this count can be shortened to:

One—lift knee and pivot.

Two—extend foot and snap it back quickly, keeping knee high.

Three—resume stance.

Eventually, the count can be shortened to "one" for the entire kick sequence.

6. Use pads for contact practice. Football dummies, Oregon shield pads, batakas, wall mats, rubber balls suspended on strings as targets, and other similar items are useful in practicing hitting, kicking, and blocking. If you don't have professional equipment, improvise. Make your own.

7. End each class session with more practice on the basic moves of kicks, strikes, and blocks. A person's skill in using the basic defensive moves determines the effectiveness of her defense. Practice until the basics become automatic.

8. Follow the schedule of lessons. If possible during practice sessions, videotape students in mock-attack situations for student viewing and self-analysis of strengths and weaknesses. If video is not available, give oral critiques of students defending themselves.

EXAMINATIONS

Substitute the following practical examination for Lessons 19 and 20 outlined in "Schedule of Lessons." The practical examination will take about two hours. If your class periods cannot be adjusted to accommodate this, the examination or the scheduling must be modified.

1. Answer twenty objective questions (true-false, multiple choice, fill-in)   *25 points*
2. Write suggested behavior for self-defense in the five dangerous situations listed during the first class session   *15 points*
3. Demonstrate the basic techniques—kicks, strikes, and (optional) throws   *20 points*
4. Demonstrate successful self-defense in four out of five attack situations—chokes and grabs, defense from ground, striking and kicking attacks, nonviolent attacks, weapon attacks

      40 points

It is also helpful if you can videotape the final demonstrations. The examination of defense in attack situations can be handled in various ways. You may wish to have students work in pairs; you may wish to be the "attacker" yourself; or you may find it helpful to have an expert in self-defense for women evaluate the students' defenses to his "attacks." The last is recommended only if you have worked closely with this expert prior to the final exam. He should know exactly what has been taught in the class, and the students must know how much contact he anticipates in their defensive moves.

SELF-DEFENSE AIDS

AUDIOVISUAL AIDS

The following films are helpful to a total program of self-defense. Each is useful for students in junior or senior high school, for college students, and for adults. Information about availability and fees can be obtained from the addresses listed.

Nobody's Victim
20 minutes, 16 mm, color
Ramsgate Films
704 Santa Monica Blvd.
Santa Monica, CA 90401

Invitations to Burglary (starring Raymond Burr)
20 minutes, 16 mm, color
Free with return postage and insurance paid
Western Insurance Information Service
1200 N. Main St.
Suite 330
Santa Ana, CA 92701
or 582 Market St.
Suite 607
San Francisco, CA 94104

Lady Beware
17 minutes, 16 mm, Super 8 mm or video-cassette, color
Pyramid Films
Box 1048
Santa Monica, CA 90406

PROTECTIVE EQUIPMENT FOR PRACTICE

The following equipment is useful in practice, especially for putting more force behind your moves without hurting your partner. If you have this equipment, fine, but you can improvise and come up with home-made items that will serve your purpose. A rag-filled laundry bag, for example, makes a good punching bag. You might also check with a football coach at a local school to see if he will share some of his equipment.

PROTECTIVE EQUIPMENT FOR PRACTICE

Oregon shield

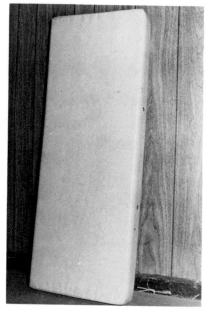

California shield

Tackling dummy

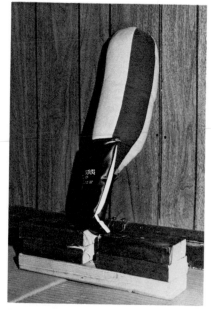

Batakas

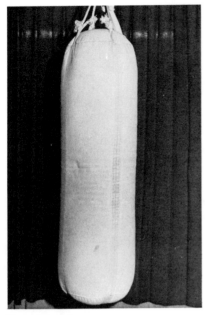

Punching bag

Hand pads

Forearm blocking shield